WELSH MINERS MUSEUM
AT AFAN ARGOED COUNTR

An illustrated guide to the history of the industry, to the development of the communities and to life in the valleys of South Wales.

Written by Afan Powell, Chairman, Welsh Miners' Museum Committee, September 1977.

First re-print September 1979.
Second re-print, with minor revisions, February 1983.
Third re-print, December 1984.

IBSN 0 907599 05 2

Introduction

The Welsh Miners' Museum at Afan Argoed Country Park, which received the Prince of Wales Award for 1976, was opened in June of that year and followed four years of endeavour by local people. Interest in the creation of a Museum in the Afan Valley arose from the fact that it had been formerly a busy mining valley with important railway connections to the coast and to other South Wales mining valleys. During the 1960's, however, a number of pit closures had taken place, the last being Glyncorrwg Colliery in 1970. With the consequent ending of mining, the region's primary industry, there arose concern over the future of the combined communities of the Afan Valley which had been very much built upon the foundation of coal. So in 1971 the then Glamorgan County Council established, with the aid of Home Office support, a Community Development Project to study the problems of the area and to foster possible new initiatives. At a public meeting convened by C.D.P. at Glyncorrwg in 1972, the idea was born to create a museum wherein the story of miners and their families, their struggle and achievements, could be told. A Museum committee was formed which worked towards that end, and with help from many people and various organisations (in particular the new West Glamorgan County Council), the museum has been established at Afan Argoed. It is hoped that it will serve as an education for all visitors.

The Welsh Miners' Museum emblem

Coal-mining & the Industrial Revolution

One could say that the story of the Coal Industry began at Coalbrookdale in Shropshire, for it was there, over two hundred years ago that Abraham Darby successfully first put coal to an important new use which did much to usher in the Industrial Revolution that so transformed the world. By using coke made from coal, instead of using charcoal obtained from the dwindling number of trees in this country, he produced good quality iron more cheaply and in greater quantities than had ever been possible before. This revolutionary process supplied the ever-growing demand for iron for the machines of the emergent factory age, for construction work, for the cannon of wars to come and for the railways and ships of the following century. So coal mining became a major industry in connection with iron making, and at later stages of the Industrial Revolution provided the fuel for the steam power age, and the raw materials for new chemical industries.

The significance of South Wales lies in the abundant supply of both iron ore and coal that was to be found beneath its wooded hills and valleys. The exploitation of these resources was to mean the transformation of the area.

The North Rhondda Colliery at Glyncorrwg, 1908.

The South Wales Coalfield

The coalfield consists of many layers or seams of coal or different thicknesses and quality, often broken and distorted. It is in the form roughly of an elongated pear-shaped basin approximately 900 square miles in area stretching from Pontypool in the east to St. Bride's Bay in the west, a distance of about ninety miles. Its widest part in Glamorgan is about twenty miles. A considerable area in the west lies beneath the seas of Swansea and Carmarthen Bays.

There are three main types of coal with many gradations between. Generally speaking, the eastern part and southern edge of the coalfield yields bituminous coal which has a high volatile content and is good for coking and household fires. The middle part of the coalfield and the lower seams yield the steam coal which fuelled the steam power age. In the western regions of the coalfield the bright hard anthracite is found which provides the fiercest heat.

In addition to the northern and southern outcrop of the coalfield basin there are many outcrops on the hills which overlook the narrow valleys of South Wales. Through these valley floors pits have been sunk to reach the deep coal of the central basin.

Male colliery worker, 1860.

Development of the Coalfield

By the eighteenth century coal mining was already on the increase in South Wales. There were shipments of coal from small ports by coastal vessels to Ireland and the West of England. Along the coast there were also expanding copper and other non-ferrous smelting industries, ores being obtained from Cornwall and West and North Wales. These industries required coal in increasing quantities.

The hills at this time were being denuded of trees, the timber being used increasingly for shipbuilding and making charcoal for iron smelting which was soon to become a major industry in the area of the northern outcrop of the South Wales coalfield. There, in the region of Merthyr Tydfil and Dowlais between Pontypool and Hirwaun, from about 1760 to 1850 was to be found the world's greatest iron making enterprises. At first using the available trees for charcoal and the fast-flowing streams for power to provide the blast of air into furnaces, the locally abundant supplies of iron ore were exploited. Later, the change over to the Darby method of iron making and the use of steam power in place of water-wheels was facilitated by the immense supplies of coal in the area.

There were fortunes to be made. Wealthy entrepreneurs from England became the famous, and infamous, iron masters. At this time agricultural land was being enclosed and people came into South Wales from other parts of rural Wales, from neighbouring English Counties and from Ireland to find work in new industries and to settle down. It was a pioneering time of gruelling work and hardship in what were usually very primitive conditions. Townships sprang up, canals

Underground haulier of the 1920's.

were constructed to connect with the coast, and tramroads were built to connect with the canals. Some time later, in the nineteenth century, when steam power was applied to transport in the form of railways and steam ships, there came about a huge and world wide demand for steam coal. So the railways began to penetrate the valleys where the steam coal was, and new docks were built to cope with the trade. From Cardiff, Newport, Barry, Port Talbot and Swansea, millions of tons of coal were to be exported annually to all parts of the world.

The first truck of coal from South Pit Colliery, Glyncorrwg, 1906.

Aerial view of Port Talbot and Aberafan c.1915.

The export of coal from Cardiff reached its peak shortly before the start of the First World War.

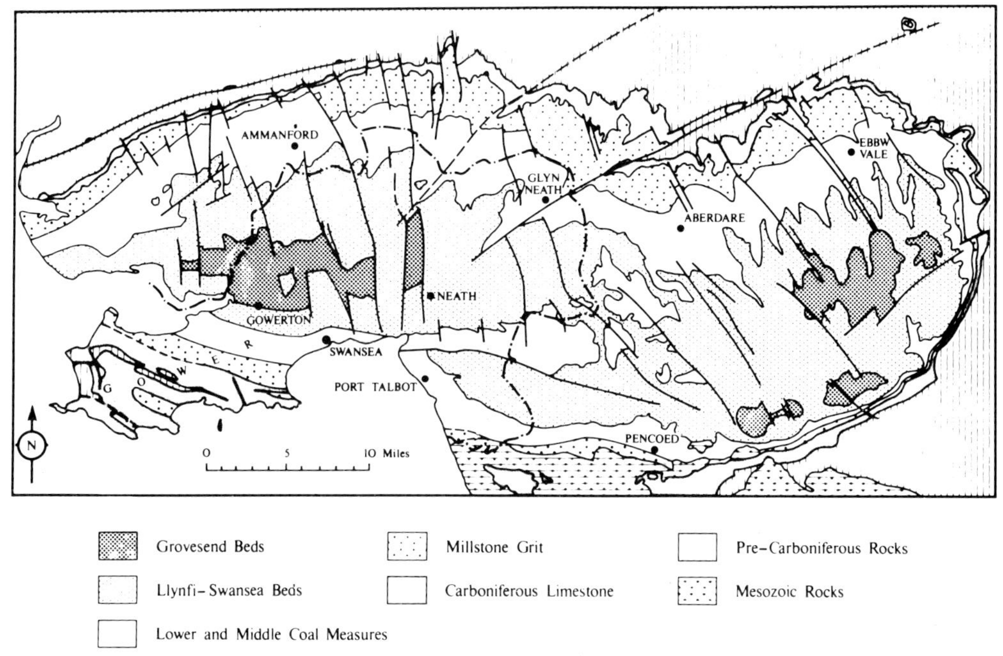

Map of the South Wales coalfield

Geological map of the South Wales Coalfield.

The main expansion of the steam coal trade took place during and after the 1870's, by which time the technical problems of the application of steam power to ships were largely solved. At that time also the once dominant iron industries inland were in decline, and the future was to see most of steel making in coastal areas where ships' plates were now commonly made and where a vast tinplate industry was developing, the bulk of the iron ore used now being imported from abroad. South Wales had become highly industrialised. Besides the steel making there were coke ovens and 'by-products' plants which yielded gas and other basic materials for many new chemical industries, including the bonding substances for the making of patent fuel briquettes from small coal. In time, Cardiff became the world's premier coal exporting port and Swansea became the world's metallurgical centre. Concomitant with this industrial power and appetite for raw materials and markets came the expansion of the British Empire.

There were many changes imminent, however. Other countries established their own industries based upon their raw materials and the copper and tinplate industries of Wales were seriously affected. In the coalfield there was also much labour unrest during the first years of this century and the technical problems of mining more deeply and extensively were increasing. Yet production rose to reach a peak of nearly 57 million tons in the year 1913, of which over 34 million tons were exported. That year also saw this country's worst ever mining disaster when 439 men died in the Senghenydd explosion. Then, after years of international tension and rivalry, came the 1914-1918 war. The position was never to be the same again for the South Wales mining industry.

Tram emerging from Blaencregan Drift Mine, which closed in 1972.

The work of Mining

In order to get coal from underground men had to dig for it. The earliest methods involved tunnelling into outcropping seams or else into hillsides until accessible seams were reached. These were the drift mines. Where coal lay in shallow seams, under flatter ground, bell-pits were sunk, the coal being wound up by hand or by horse gins.

As mining became deeper, the problems associated with it became greater. Roof and side falls had to be countered by timber supports and packing. There were problems of drainage of water and it was not until Newcomen's engine in the early 18th century that pumping became feasible. Ventilation problems to remove or dilute foul air and noxious gases that were stifling or inflammable had to be overcome. Naked flames to provide lighting caused many explosions and efforts to solve this difficulty led to the Davy Safety lamp of 1815.

The actual getting of coal was by means of pick and shovel work, the coal being put into wooden tubs that were dragged to the surface in the early days by women and children. Restrictions on their employment were not introduced until the 1842 Mines Act which followed an official investivation. The years that followed saw the beginning of the inspection of mines which slowly and with difficulty brought about a greater degree of safety and education in mining practice. Horses were used a great deal for haulage underground now. Ventilation of pits was often by means of furnace induced draughts!

A 1950's view of Glyncorrwg, a typical South Wales mining community.

A selection of underground equipment and machinery : (i) Various miners' lamps; (ii) Huwood Boring Machine with Dust Suppressor (1944); (iii) The Flint Wheel, an early form of producing light in the mines; (v) Supporting props within the Coal Seam. (iv) One of the first Diamond Disc Machines (1894);

By hard experience the engineering techniques of mining developed. Steam power was used for winding engines and haulage. Wire ropes were made. Compressed air power came to be used for haulage and the drilling machines which made the holes to receive the blasting explosives that were used. Steam powered air pumps were developed and, later, large powerful fans. Electricity began to be used for lighting and for powering early coal cutting machines and conveyors.

At the beginning of this century, after the terrible disaster at Courriers in France in 1906, the first rescue stations were established where men were trained in the use of breathing apparatus and first aid.

All the while thousands of men continued to use mandrels, shovels and "curling boxes", and "sledge and wedge", in cramped positions and often lying on their sides (soaking wet also in many drift mines). They were constantly on the alert for danger and for falls and "squeezes", because the geological conditions in South Wales were very difficult. Such was the work of mining, in poor light which caused the eye trouble of nystagmus, and in dust laden atmosphere which was bound to ruin the miner's lungs and lead to painful and premature death.

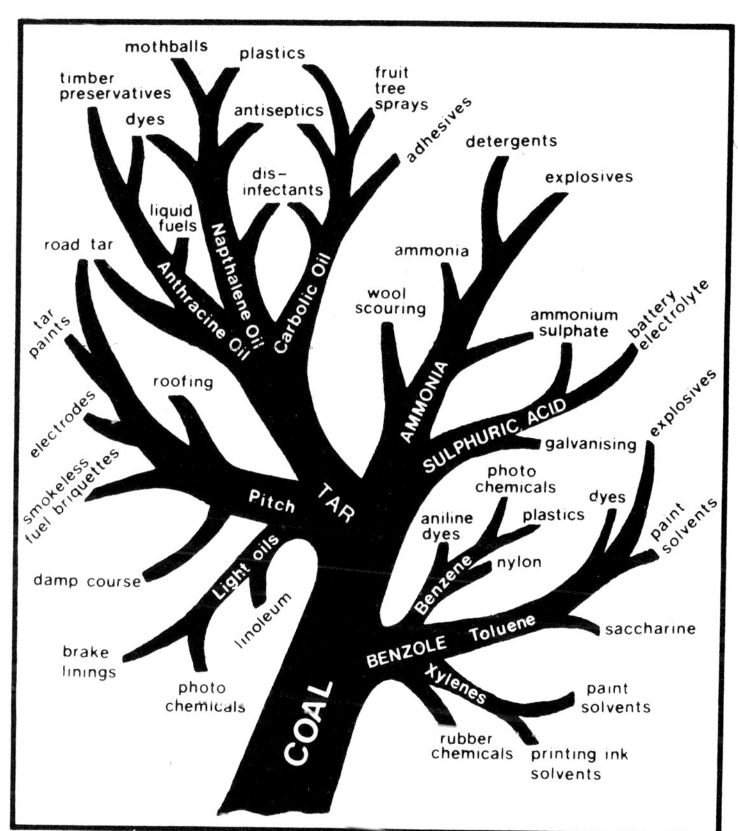

Diagram showing the by-products of coal.

Explosions in the Mines

Although it must be remembered that the great majority of accidents in the mines were in connection with falls of roof or sides, haulage, or at shafts, it is understandable that it was the incidence of explosions in collieries which made the deepest impact on the minds of people. The gassy nature and dustiness of many pits in South Wales created a bad record. Thirteen of the twenty seven major disasters from explosions in Great Britain between 1890 and 1913 took place in South Wales, with the loss of 1465 men. Better ventilation was vital in order to overcome the problems. Ignition of an explosive mixture of fire-damp (methane) and air was possible from any of the following causes: spontaneous heating of coal, overheated surfaces, naked flames, friction sparks, electric sparks, use of explosives, sparking from steel upon steel or stone, sparking from stones falling upon stones. A drop in air pressure above ground meant a greater emission of pent up gas below, especially from the much disturbed strata of South Wales. The dilution and cooling of the mine atmosphere was essential. An adequate flow of air had to be drawn in through the mine workings and this flow had to be measured, guided and controlled constantly. Men learned to judge the presence of gas by carefully studying its effect

Miner undercutting coal with the use of a naked flame, 1905.

upon the flame of a safety lamp. With scientific progress various types of gas detectors were developed.

Another hazard was that fine coal dust in the air in sufficient quantities was in itself explosive without the presence of gas, and could terribly increase the effect of any initial explosion of firedamp. So the suppression of dust became a major concern in mining. Spraying with water and infusing it with drilling machines were some methods used, and attempts were made to keep roadways clean. It was eventually realised that the presence of an

Wives, mothers and children waiting in hope after a pit explosion; a scene once only too familiar in South Wales.

Underground fireman practising early method of getting rid of firedamp.

inert stone dust, e.g. limestone, eliminated the explosiveness of coal dust, and it is the practice today to stone-dust vulnerable areas in volatile seams.

The worst ever explosion in British mining took place in 1913 at Senghenydd, when 439 men were killed, many from suffocation after the disaster.

Although it was known to be a dangerous pit (81 men died in the 1901 explosion there) there were many infringements of safety precautions by the management and owners. This was revealed in the Court of Enquiry which the Home Office instituted with seeming reluctance in 1914. Among these infringements were failure to clear away dust, to provide reversible air flow in an emergency, to sample the mine's atmosphere and to measure air currents. No director of the company was called to the enquiry and there was no final agreement as to the actual cause of the explosion.

The scene at Senghenydd following Britain's worst mining disaster on October 13th, 1913.

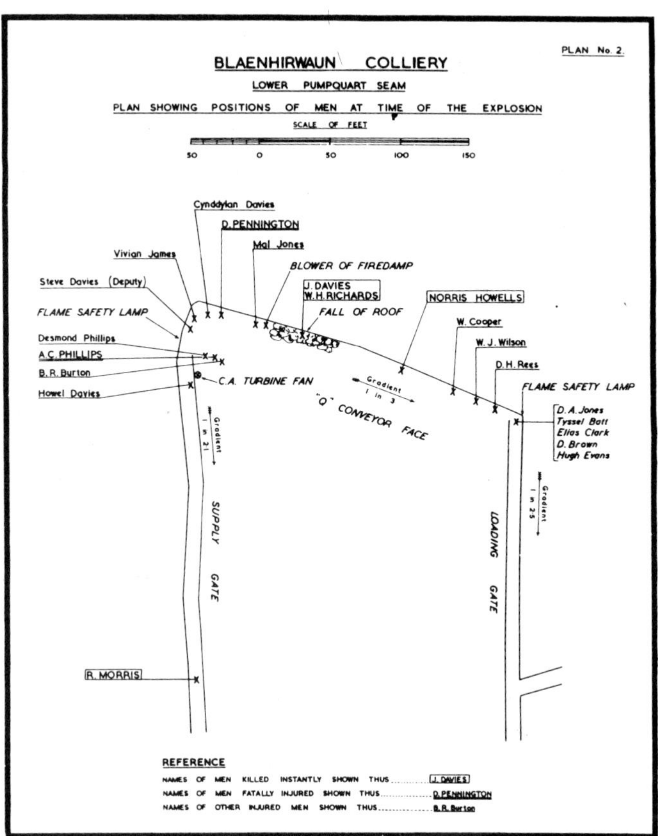

Detail plan showing the aftermath of the explosion at Blaenhirwaun Colliery in 1955 in which six men died.

Mining Communities

The people who came from various parts of Britain to work in the expanding iron and coal industries had to adapt not only to new ways of working but to new communities. They had to discover how to live together. There were problems of integration to be overcome, and sometimes antipathy among the Welsh, English and Irish. It must be remembered too that the Welsh language was the first, sometimes the only, language among the Welsh people who formed the bulk of the population in the early days. But the people shared a common work experience and slowly there was forged an awareness of shared identity and destiny. Living conditions at first were primitive, and the long hours of backbreaking toil in hazardous and often brutalising conditions did not help towards refinement of feelings. The harsh circumstances inevitably engendered protest and action. Radical political attitudes vied with religious influences in efforts to seek improvements. Working people had to learn how to associate together in new ways to cope with their problems, meeting with success and failure at different times. The nineteenth century saw the beginning of trade union associations, the formation of Benefit Societies and the building of chapels of various denominations.

Housing was in short supply and, besides speculative building and company houses, self-building clubs were formed. Large families were common and many homes had lodgers. There was a high mobility of labour among young men from area to area.

Group of colliers at the mine entrance.

With bad sanitation and shared privies it is no wonder that there were outbreaks of cholera in the mid-century. What little education there was came from the efforts of voluntary organisations, religious Sunday Schools and from some schools provided by a few enlightened employers. The latter part of the nineteenth century was to see

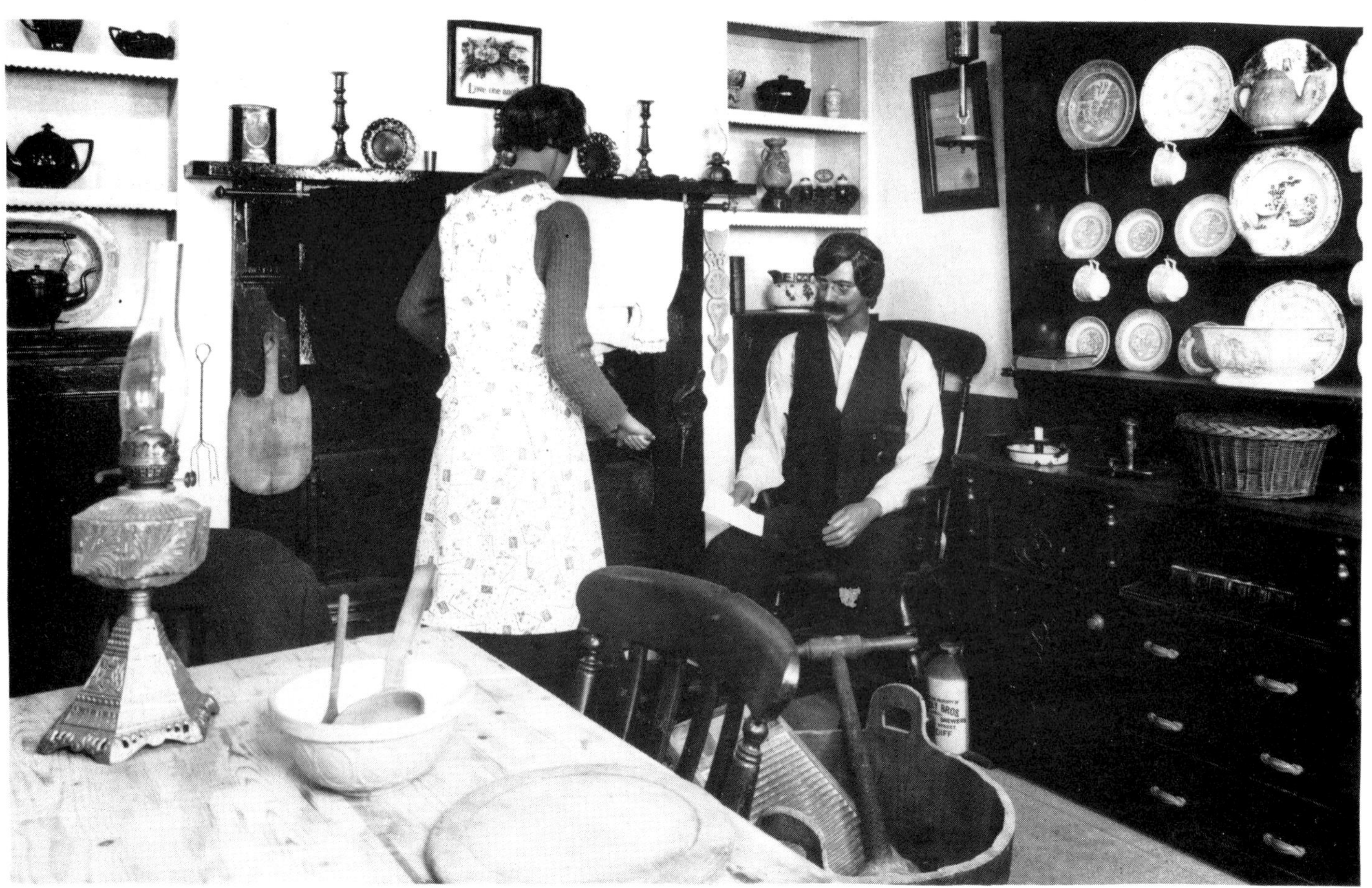

Part of the Domestic Scene at the Miners' Museum.

great improvement in living conditions through new forms of local government and the introduction of state education.

The vigour of the communities found expression in many sports also, and the present day passion for rugby football in Wales speaks for its early popularity. Life was not a tale of unrelieved hardship. The people entertained themselves, made their own music with drum and fife bands, and there would be carnivals at times.

The role of the noncomformist religious bodies deserves special mention in the story of the industrial communities of Wales. Religion was a powerful influence. Long eloquent sermons were listened to avidly and hymns fervently sung in four part harmony by working men and their families. The Tonic Sofa system of musical notation was eagerly learned and Wales became famous for its choirs, for the Gymanfa Ganu or singing festival, and for the Eisteddfod. The chapels saved the Welsh language from extinction in industrial South Wales, fostered dramas and cantatas in the vestries and generated the strong Temperance movements opposing the intemperance that was also prevalent in the society.

The mining communities were of rich diversity and had a character of their own. In the homes joined in terraces on the hills, the women worked as hard as the men: baking, black-leading the shining grates, boiling water for tired blackened men coming home in filthy clothes from different shifts each day to bath before the fire, greasing their boots, scrubbing, washing, ironing, sewing and darning, bringing up the children. It was a way of life. The people were warm and vital. They often had to be stoic. They worked and lived together and so knew each other. They were 'belonging .

Part of a superb wood carving of a Welsh kitchen and underground scene, the work of Handel Edwards of Skewen, now in Ulster Folk Museum, Ireland.

Montage of Welsh Community Life.

Industrial Relations

The fact that the South Wales Miners' Federation, the first stable miners' trade union in South Wales, was not formed until 1898 indicates the difficulty that workmen had in establishing a sense of unity and purpose in their struggle for improvements in wages and working conditions. During the early 1800's there were spontaneous riots of protest among ironworkers at Merthyr against wage cuts and truck shop abuses. These were suppressed with the aid of the military. Colliers soon began to join cause with the ironworkers. At times of stress gangs of men would march from one area to another, seeking solidarity.

After the repeal of the Combination Laws in 1824 it became legally possible to form trade unions, but it was difficult for untutored men to organise themselves. Discontent flared into rioting at Merthyr in 1831, and later that year one of the men's leaders, Dic Penderyn, was hanged at Cardiff. He is not forgotten to this day in South Wales. At this time also there were the so called "Scotch cattle" pressure groups among workmen endeavouring to create unity against the employers. A few years later the movement of Chartism expressed the anger and frustration of working people throughout Britain. A large demonstration at Newport in 1839 was met with troops and there was resultant loss of life.

Blacklegs being escorted by police in the Garw Valley in 1928.

There were several reasons besides the repressions of employers and magistrates why associations of working men in South Wales were not lasting. There were problems of integrating the various nationalities of Welsh, English and Irish. Better

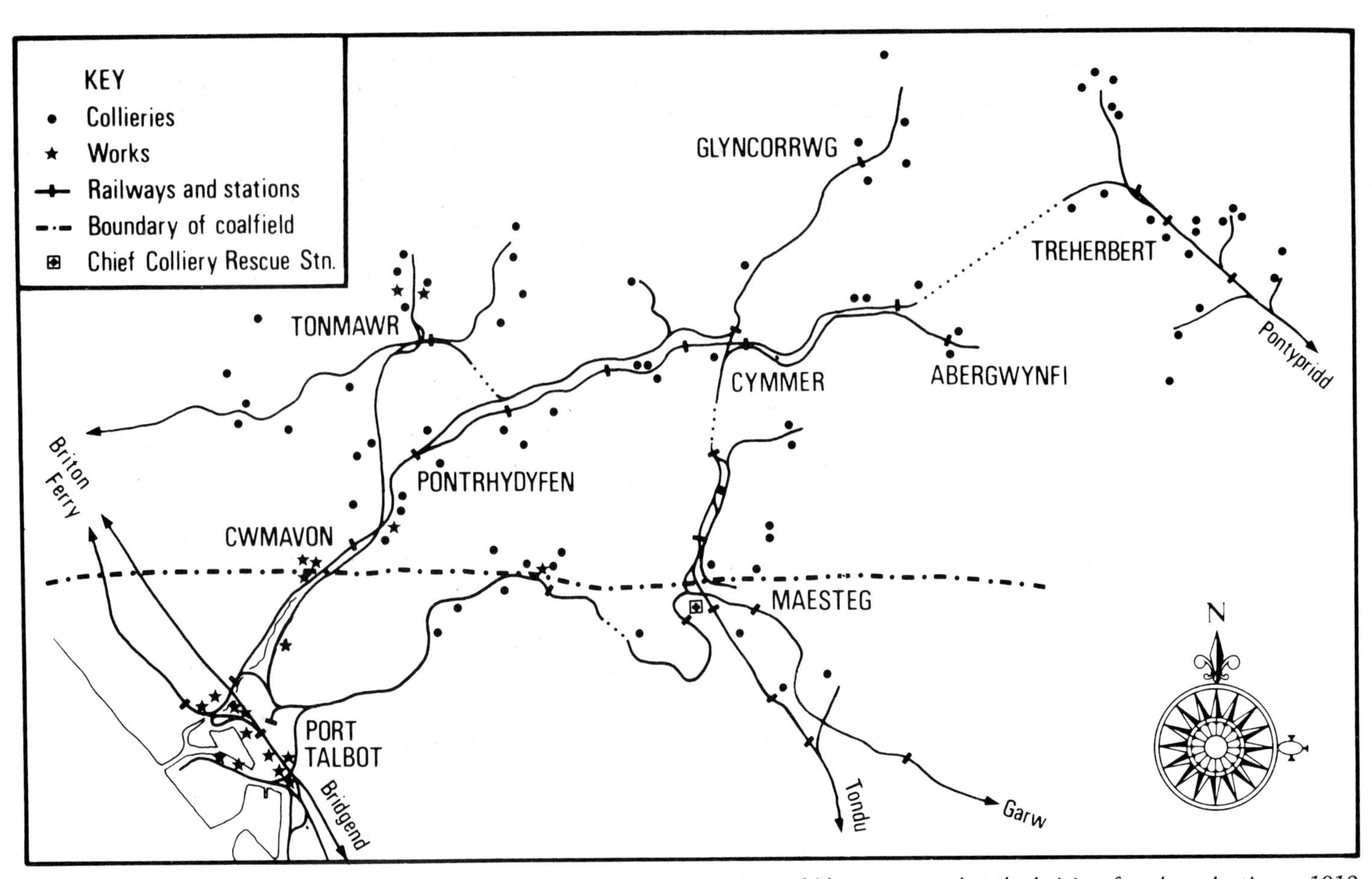

Map of the industrial Afan Valley and neighbouring areas as it would have appeared at the height of coal-production, c.1912.

established English unions found it difficult to collect dues when seeking recruits. There was the language difficulty to be overcome. Many valleys were geographically isolated. In times of stress alternative work was often available for men willing and able to move to other areas, for different types of coal enjoyed or suffered different market conditions, and iron masters competed with sale coal owners for trade and workforce. It was not until the 1870's that the coal owners themselves combined in a strong and lasting association.

The early 1880's was a time of low ebb in trade unionism in the country but it also saw the formation of several socialist societies which were to lead the way eventually to the Labour Party of today. In South Wales from 1875 to the turn of the century there was instituted a system of sliding scale agreements by which the tonnage rates paid to miners for cutting large clean coal fluctuated according to its selling price. The small coal was not allowed for! The most prominent representative of the miners in negotiation with the employers throughout this time was Willian Abraham, better known by his Bardic title of Mabon, who became M.P. for the Rhondda.

During the 1890's there were great strains in the industry. Hauliers went on strike in 1893 and the

D. DAVIS & SONS, Ltd.

FERNDALE COLLIERIES.

NOTICE!

The attention of all workmen is called to the fact that the output obtained from these Pits is so low that the question of continuing working is being seriously considered.

Unless the OUTPUT per man employed is IMMEDIATELY IMPROVED the Pits must stop.

F. LLEWELLIN JACOB,

1st November, 1921 GENERAL MANAGER

Poster urging increased productivity, one of many that were commonplace in 1921.

military were called in. Mabon the conciliator came under great pressure from the frustrated men. Out of the agitation and distress the South Wales Miners' Federation was born in 1898. Its early years were difficult and pioneering. The sliding scale agreements ended in 1902, the year after Kier Hardie was elected M.P. for Merthyr. The new union now engaged in fierce struggles with the employers over issues of the eight hour day, allowances for working in abnormal places where a man could not get enough coal out to earn a living wage and, later on, the fight for a minimum wage. At times there was great unrest and again the military appeared on the scene. Syndicalist ideas of workers control and ownership of the mines began to gain ground. Then came the first World War.

The period following was a very difficult one for the Welsh coal trade. Besides the dislocation of trade there was a loss of previous markets made worse by German reparations in the form of coal to France and Italy, hitherto among our best customers. And, of profound importance, oil began to replace coal as fuel for shipping. There was poverty, depression and resistance against wage cuts and a longer working day being imposed. The 1917 upheavals in Russia created ripples in British society. 1921 and the 1926 General Strike which the miners continued alone for seven months to ultimate submission are dates of grim memory. Then followed the years of the depression in the 1930's. There was much unemployment. Many men left South Wales to seek work elsewhere. They were hard and bitter times, with growing conflict between ideas of fascism and communism in the world. The libraries of the Miners' Institutes and Workingmen's Halls which had been built from the men's weekly contributions served to educate those who sought to understand the events and circumstances of the time. These institutes were also the focal points of assembly in the villages, where concerts and dramas were held, billiards played, and where the local cinema would sometimes be housed.

Through the Lodge Committees of their union, the miners made efforts to improve conditions of work and remuneration and fought for the claims for compensation made by men suffering from injury from accident or from the dreaded chest diseases of silicosis and pneumoconiosis.

The coal trade began to revive in the late 1930's but in 1939 came the dislocation of the Second World War, during which there was conscription of men to the mines. By 1945 the coal industry was ill-fitted after years of lack of capital investment to face the post war world and there was no other course to follow but to nationalise it, which the new Labour Government did in 1947.

A contrast in collieries as the demand for coal declines and mining becomes more mechanised and straightforward. The former colliery at Glyncorrwg (left), is typical of the traditional-style colliery. It was reconstructed in 1960, and closed in 1970. By comparison Abernant, near Pontardawe (right), is a semi-modern anthracite plant, built in 1958, and is virtually a hundred percent mechanised.

The National Coal Board & the Future

The National Coal Board set about the tremendous task of rescuing and revitalising the coal industry. A programme of modernisation and mechanisation began, training schools established for new recruits and pit head baths built extensively to improve the life of the miner.

Dyffryn Rhondda in the early 1930's, showing the remains of Nant-y-Bar cottages in the foreground and the old gasworks on the left.

But many uneconomic pits were closed and there were to be other factors in the post war world which were to threaten the coal industry. Prospects of nuclear power and North Sea gas and cheap abundant oil reduced the status of coal and during the 1960's there were many further pit closures, sometimes even after massive amounts of money had been injected into them. Morale in the industry and in the mining communities understandably declined. Men sought work in other industries, absenteeism was high, and efforts to mechanise mining in many South Wales pits proved difficult because of geological disturbances.

However, the fortunes of coal have changed. The difficulties of obtaining nuclear power, long term doubts regarding continuing supplies of gas and oil from the North Sea and, most important, the new Arab awareness of the value and significance of their oil to the World economy have transformed our regard for coal, on which our original industrial greatness was built. Today, we have been taught to look upon it with new respect, for without a doubt we shall depend upon it for a very long time to come.

The Afan Valley & District

There could be no greater contrast than that which exists between the peacefulness of the Afan Valley at Argoed and the industrial activity of Port Talbot, only six miles away, which is dominated by the blast furnaces and strip mills of the British Steel Corporation. Today, big ships discharge their cargoes of iron ore at the deep water harbour there, to feed the hungry furnaces. To the west, on what was once moorland, there is a vast petro-chemical works which at night-time seems to be a fairyland of lights. How did all this industry begin? We must go back over two hundred years to find out.

Evening-time view of the modern B.P. Chemicals complex at Baglan Bay.

The rise of industry began locally with the establishing of a copper works at Taibach in 1770 for the smelting of ores received from Cornwall and North Wales. This led to more intensive exploration and entering of the coal resources of the nearby hills which had already been largely denuded trees, and from which only slight quantities of coal had previously been taken. This copper works was expanded in 1800 with the installation of rolling mills, new furnaces and a 100 h.p. steam engine.

Industrial activity increased in the early years of the nineteenth century with the building of tin-plate works at Aberavon, but it was to be in the Cwmavon region that the next great developments were to take place. An ironworks there in 1819 was followed by a tinplate works in 1825. Then, at Pontrhydyfen, in 1827, another ironworks was built and, connected with it, a fine aqueduct which today serves as a viaduct. By 1835 a copper works to rival the one at Taibach had been built at Cwmavon, and the remains of the flue which led away the poisonous fumes up the side of the mountain to a stack at the top can be seen today.

The stack, known locally as "Stac-y-Foel" stood for over one hundred years like a sentinel above the village until it was demolished in 1940. Inevitably there was an influx of people into the area, and the language and culture of the expanding community was predominantly Welsh. William Abraham, to be known more famously as "Mabon", the foremost miners' leader in the latter part of the nineteenth century, was born at Cwmavon in 1842.

Eleven years previously, in 1831, an earlier champion of working men, Dic Penderyn, was laid to rest at St. Mary's Church in Aberavon. It was at Aberavon and nearby Taibach that further significant developments took place. In 1836 the course of the River Afan was altered, a docks created, and the name Port Talbot officially adopted to commemorate C.R.M. Talbot of Margam Castle. The ensuing years saw increasing activity. The ill-fated Morfa Pit was sunk by 1849 and by 1850 there was a gasworks at Aberavon and the South Wales Railway had arrived. At Taibach in 1864 another gasworks was built and the copper works continued against the competition at Cwmavon. Over the next twenty years several tinplate works were established in the growing town of Port Talbot. The fortunes of tinplate and copper were to decline, however, in the 1890's and at the turn of the century, but at the same time new enterprises were undertaken at the town which were to be of great long term significance. The Port Talbot Docks and Railway Company was formed which extended the docks and sent lines into the hinterland to bring more coal and industry to the port. In 1901 the Port Talbot Steelworks was built, to be followed in the middle of the First World War by the Margam Steelworks, which laid the basis for the more modern strip mills built at Margam at the end of the Second World War.

The turn of the century also saw much activity in the upper Afan Valley, with a continued expansion of mining and several new pits being sunk. The Rhondda and Swansea Bay Railway had been constructed in the 1880's from Port Talbot, and connections to Treorchy from Blaengwynfi and to Maesteg from Cymmer had been made by tunnels under the mountains. It was not the first railway in the valley, however; by 1863 the South Wales Mineral Railway had reached Glyncorrwg from Briton Ferry, entering the valley through the Gyfylchi Tunnel from Tonmawr at a point opposite the Afan Argoed Country Park Centre. This had given great impetus to the mining in the Glyncorrwg area which had already begun above Blaencregan, from where coal had been taken by the Parson's Folly tramroad to a tipple on the bank of the Neath Canal. Throughout the latter half of the nineteenth century, until the First World War, the upper Afan Valley was developed. Millions of tons of coal were taken out of the hills and from the deep pits and transported by rail. A brick-works at Argoed used clay from the nearby mines. A gas works was built near Duffryn Rhondda Pit. At Nantewlaeth Pit a patent fuel briquetting plant was built.

After the First World War the area suffered, in common with many other places, from the difficulties and disturbances of the 1920's and 1930's. After the 1939-45 War came the nationalisation of the mines. Over the years since then mining has ceased in the vicinity of Port Talbot and in the upper Afan Valley, although a great deal of money was injected into some pits. The last to close was Glyncorrwg Colliery in 1970. Two years later came the idea of the Miners' Museum which was to find its home at the Afan Argoed Country Park. There, amid the peace and beauty of the forest-clad hills, with only the old tips and railway tracks as silent reminders of the past, visitors may learn something of the story of coal.

In Loving Memory

OF THE

MINERS WHO LOST THEIR LIVES

— IN —

WELSH COLLIERY DISASTERS

	Killed.
1934—September 22, Gresford, Wrexham	261
1932—January 25, Llwynypia, Rhondda	11
1931—Aug. 25, Caerau, Mountain Out-crop	3
1929—July 10, Milfraen, Blaenavon	9
1929—Nov. 28, Wernbwll, nr. Penclawdd	7
1927—March 1, Cwm, Ebbw Vale	52
1923—April 26th, Trimsaran	9
1913—October 13, Senghenydd	436
1905—July 5, Wattstown	119
1905—March 10, Clydach Vale	31
1901—September 10, Llanbradach	12
1901—May 24, Senghenydd	82
1899—August 18, Llest Colliery, Garw	19
1896—January 28, Tylorstown	57
1894—June 25, Cilfynydd	276
1892—August 26, Park Slip	110
1892—Aug. 12, Great Western Colliery	58
1890—March 8, Morfa	87
1890—February 6, Llanerch	176
1890—January 20, Glyn Pit, Pontypool	5
1888—May 14, Aber, Tynewydd	5
1887—February 18, Ynyshir	37
1885—December 24, Mardy	81
1885—Naval Colliery	14
1884—Nov. 8,. Pochin Colliery, Tredegar	14
1884—January 28, Penygraig	11
1884—January 16, Cwmavon	10
1883—August 21, Gelli	4
1883—February 1, Coedcae	5
1883—February 11, Coedcae	6
1882—January 15, Risca	4
1880—Dec. 10, Naval Steam Colliery	96
1880—July 15, Risca	119
1879—Sept. 22, Waunllwyd, Ebbw Vale	84
1879—January 13, Dinas	3
1878—September 11, Abercarn	268

	Killed.
1878—September 1, Abercarn	62
1877—March 8, Worcester Pit, Swansea	18
1876—December 13, Abertillery	20
1875—December 5, Llan Pit, Pentyrch	12
1875—December 4, New Tredegar	22
1874—July 24, Charles Pit, Llansamlet	19
1874—April 5, Abertillery	6
1872—March 8, Wernfach	18
1872—March 2, Victoria	19
1872—Jan. 10, Oakwood, Llynvi Valley	11
1871—October 4, Gelli Pit, Aberdare	4
1871—February 24, Pentre	38
1870—July 23, Llansamlet	19
1869—June 10, Ferndale	60
1869—May 23, Llanerch	7
1867—November 8, Ferndale	178
1865—December 20, Upper Gethin	30
1865—June 16, Tredegar	2
1863—December 24, Maesteg	14
1863—October 17, Margam	39
1862—February 19, Gethin, Merthyr	47
1860—December 1, Risca	146
1859—April 5, Neath Chain Colliery	26
1858—October 13, Duffryn	20
1856—July 13, Cymmer	114
1853—March 12, Risca Vale	10
1852—May 10, Duffryn	64
1850—Dec. 14, New Duffryn Colliery	13
1849—Aug. 11, Lletty Shenkin, Aberdare	52
1848—June 21, Victoria (Mon.)	11
1846—January 14, Risca	35
1845—August 2, Cwmbach	28
1844—January 1, Dinas	12
1837—June 17, Blaina (Mon.)	21
1837—May 10, Plas-yr-Argoed, Mold	21

"IN THE MIDST OF LIFE WE ARE IN DEATH."

Let's hope the Gallant Miners havn't died in vain,
On God's own shore their friends might meet them once again.

C. P., TR.]

Museum plan & Information

Opening hours :
April - October : Daily 10.30 - 18.00
November - March : Saturdays & Sundays 10.30 - 17.00

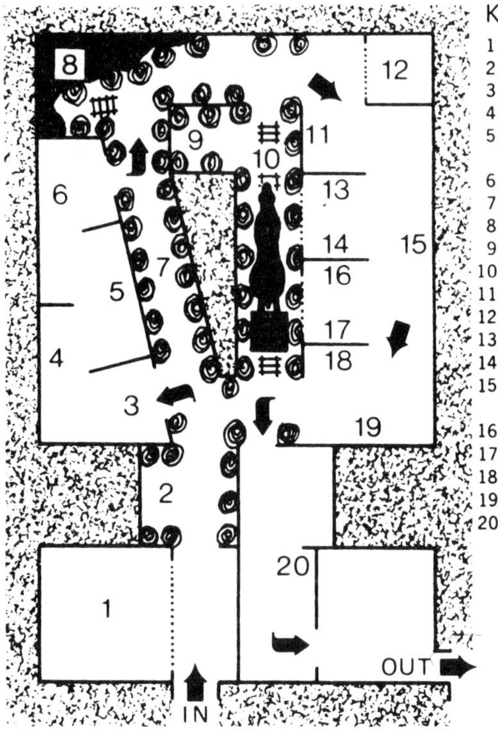

KEY TO PLAN

1. Domestic scene
2. Lamp station
3. Uses of coal
4. Early mining
5. Women and children in the mines
6. Coal-getting
7. In-take roadway
8. Simulated mine working
9. Underground stable
10. Return roadway
11. Colliery disasters
12. Mine rescue
13. Surface transport
14. Pit winding engines
15. Community and Mineworkers' Union
16. War-time activities
17. Sport and recreation
18. Modern mining
19. Pneumoconiosis
20. Bi-products

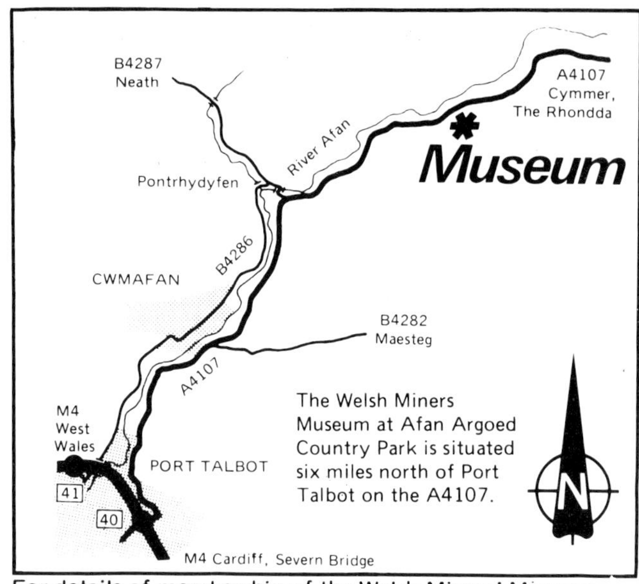

For details of membership of the Welsh Miners' Museum Committee, its aims and objectives, and further information, contact :

Mr. Richard Phillips (Chairman)
18 Brytwn Road, Cymmer, Port Talbot.
Tel : Cymmer 850971.

Mr. Glyn Thomas (Secretary)
16 Percy Road, Cynonville, Port Talbot.
Tel : Cymmer 850875.